Pharmacy Law Review by Sharon D. Garrett, CPhT

Published by Sharon Denise Garrett, C
201 Rue Beauregard
Suite 202
Lafayette, LA, 70508
gpsrxla@gmail.com

Cover by Canva and Sharon D. Garrett, CPhT

Disclaimer notice:

Please note the information contained within this document is for educational and entertainment purposes only. All efforts have been executed to present accurate, up to date, reliable, and complete information. No warranties of any kind are declared or implied. Readers acknowledge that the author is not engaging in rendering of legal, financial, medical, or professional advice. The content within this book has been derived from various sources. Please consult a licensed professional before attempting any techniques outlined in this book.

By reading this document, the reader agrees that under no circumstances is the author responsible for any losses, direct or indirect, which are incurred as a result of the use of the information contained within this document, including, but not limited to, --- errors, omissions, or inaccuracies.

This page was intended to be blank

Table of Content

Pharmacy Laws

- **Federal Food and Drug Act of 1906 (Pure Food and Drug Act of 1906)**- Prohibits the sale of adulterated or mislabeled food, drinks, and drugs. This ensured that products were safe for consumption and all ingredients were listed on the product.

- **Sherley Amendment of 1912**- Prohibit false therapeutic claims. Medicines must do what the seller or manufacturer says it is going to do for the consumer.

- **Harrison Narcotic Act of 1914**- This act limited the transportation and purchase of Opium. To purchase Opium, a physician must write a prescription.

- **Food, Drug, and Cosmetic Act of 1938 (FDCA of 1938)**- This act was added language to the FDA of 1906, and now includes cosmetics. Products must include patient specific medication labels, package inserts, all drugs must be proven safe according to the FDA guidelines, and addictive drugs must be labeled as: "may be habit forming."

- **Durham Humphrey Amendment of 1951 (DHA of 1951)**- This act defined what category drugs went into. They were either behind the counter (BTC) or over the counter (OTC). Behind the counter drugs are now called legend drugs and can only be purchased under physician's supervision. Manufacturers were required to add a caution label on their medication bottles: "***Caution: Federal law prohibits dispensing without a prescription***". Over the counter drugs were required to have the product name, manufacturers name and address, active ingredients, and quantity of all ingredients (active or inactive), if they were not under the supervision of a physician.

Pharmacy Laws

- **Kefauver-Harris Amendment of 1962 (Drug Efficacy Amendment of 1962)**- All drugs produced in or after 1938 must prove that they are safe and effective for consumption. This amendment was created due to birth defects from the drug Thalidomide in Europe. This created good manufacturing practices (GMP). This placed strict quality control systems on manufacturers to ensure the consistency of their products. Manufacturers had to also gain drug approval before marketing a drug and the Federal Trade Commission (FTC) were now responsible for drug advertising. Manufacturers are required to be inspected every 2 years, report any adverse reactions, and register yearly with the governing agency.

- **Comprehensive Drug Abuse Prevention and Control Act of 1970 (CSA of 1970)**- The Drug Enforcement Administration (DEA) was formed and all controlled substances were now placed in categories or "schedules" according to medical usage and abuse potential. Drugs with the highest potential of abuse were to remain illegal and have no medical uses. These were labeled Schedule 1 (C-I) . Drug with the least potential of abuse were labeled Schedule 5 (C-V).

- **Poison Prevention Packaging Act of 1970**- This act required most drugs to be dispensed in child proof caps or packaging. There are drugs that are exempt from this type of packaging. *Nitroglycerin* is exempt because this drug is used in emergency situations and must be accessed quickly. Also, any drug packaged in such a small quantity that it could not harm a five-year-old child does not need to be packaged in child proof package.

- **Orphan Drug Act of 1983**- This act promotes the research and marketing of drugs needed for the treatment of rare diseases. These drugs are manufactured in low quantities because only a small percent of the public would need them.

Pharmacy Laws

- **Hatch-Waxman Act of 1984 (Drug Price Competition and Patent-Term Restoration Act of 1984)**- This act granted the approval of generic drugs. Manufacturers were giving the incentive of patent extensions if they created new drugs. Once a patent expired on an older brand name drug, generic manufacturers were able to create new, safe, and advanced medications.

- **Food and Drug Administration Act of 1988 (FDA of 1988)**- The FDA becomes an official established agency of the Department of Health and Human Services. The Prescription Drug Marketing Act was also enacted. This banned the sale, trade, or purchase of medication samples, medication coupons, and deep discounts to hospitals.

- **Omnibus Budget Reconciliation Act of 1990 (OBRA 1990)**- This act required Pharmacists to make an offer or an attempt to counsel patients on all new prescriptions. This was specifically enacted for Medicaid patients. This was to ensure Medicaid patients received proper care from their local pharmacies. This also required prescription leaflets to be issued with a patient's medication. Information such as drug names, strength, description, how much to take, quantity given to patients, refills, interactions, adverse effects, what to do if a dose is missed, and what to do in case of an overdose were all found on this leaflet. This also created the Pharmacy Technicians career field due to Pharmacists needing to perform Drug Utilization Reviews.

- **Dietary Supplement Health and Education Act of 1994-** Dietary Supplement manufacturers are prohibited from making false claims about a supplement (mislabeling or adulterated products). The FDA also took control of monitoring Dietary Supplement labels to ensure product quality and patient safety.

Pharmacy Laws

- **Health Insurance Portability and Accountability Act of 1996 (HIPAA of 1996)**- This act created rules and regulations regarding protected patient health information (PHI). This act also helps maintain the low cost of transmitting insurance claims. This act limits who has access to, distribution, and receives patient private health information. Only members of the patient's immediate healthcare team are allowed access to a patient's health information. Violations of this act may result in termination of employment.

- **FDA Modernization Act of 1997**- Allowed other forms of medication testing (non-animal testing) to gain drug approval faster. This act also removed the ***"May be habit forming"*** caution warning and replaced it with **"Rx Only"** on all manufacturers behind the counter medications.

- **Combat Methamphetamine Epidemic Act of 2006 (CMEA of 2006)**- Created a federal limit on the purchase of pseudoephedrine products . *No more than 3.6 grams per day or 9 grams per 30 days may be purchased*. Pharmacies are required to log each purchase of these products by paper or electronic log by requesting the patient's driver license or state identification.

- **Medicaid Tamper Resistant Prescription Pad law of 2008**- All prescription pads are to have tamper proof features (watermark symbols or special paper) to prevent medication diversion (theft).

- **Affordable Care Act of 2010 (Obamacare 2010)**- This act granted affordable health insurance to the uninsured and under-insured regardless of pre-existing health conditions.

Patient Medication Label

This is required by the Food, Drug, and Cosmetic Act of 1938

A patient specific medication label by federal law must contain the following:

1. Name, address, and phone number of dispensing pharmacy
2. Patient name and address
3. Physician name
4. Prescription number and date the prescription was filled
5. Name, strength, quantity, and directions for the drug
6. Name or initials of dispensing Pharmacist and/or Pharmacy Technician
7. Expiration date, refills, and any precautions
8. Statement: Federal law prohibits dispensing without a prescription
9. Circle quantity dispensed for controlled substance
10. Package inserts/ Leaflets placed in medication bags

Package Inserts

This is required by the Food, Drug, and Cosmetic Act of 1938

A package insert must contain the following information:

1. Description of drug
2. Clinical Pharmacology
3. Indication and uses
4. Interactions, precautions, warnings, and adverse reactions
5. Drug abuse, overdose, and dependence information
6. How the drug is supplied, how to take it, and dosage
7. Most recent label revision

The following medications must be dispensed with a package insert:

1. Oral Contraceptives
2. Estrogen and Progestational medications
3. Intrauterine Contraceptives
4. Accutane
5. Metered Dose Inhalers

National Drug Code (NDC)

Each drug produced by a manufacturer has a specific identifying NDC number. The NDC number contains three segments of digits, which identifies the manufacturers, drug information, and pack size. In total, a NDC number contains 11 digits. If a digit is missing in any segment, you can add a leading zero to that segment.

- **First Segment** – The first 5 digits in a NDC number identifies the manufacturer. All drugs made by the same manufacturer will have the same first 5 digits for all drugs that they manufacture.

  Example: Watson: **62037**

- **Second Segment**- The next 4 digits in a NDC number identifies the specific drug made by a manufacturer. Each drug has its own number. Drugs that have the same name, but different strengths, will have the same match first three digits in this segment.

  Example:
  Metoprolol Succinate ER 50mg – **831 or 0831**
  Metoprolol Succinate ER 100mg – **832 or 0832**

- **Last Segment**- The last two digits in a NDC number identifies the package size.

Example:
Drugs that arrive from the manufacturer in quantities of 100 tablets have the identifying digits of 01. Drugs that have the quantities of 500 tablets have the identifying digits of 05. And drugs that have the quantities of 1000 tablets have the identifying digits of 10.

Final:
Waston, Metoprolol Succinate ER 50mg #100 – **62037-0831-01**
Waston, Metoprolol Succinate ER 100mg #1000- **62037-0832-10**

DEA Forms

-DEA Form 41: This form is used to document destruction of controlled substances.

-DEA Form 106: This form is used to report the loss or theft of controlled substances. This form is used only if 5% or more of the total yearly product sold is missing. Example: If your pharmacy sells 1270 Adderall per year and 64 tablets were to go missing, DEA 106 form must be filled out and submitted by the Pharmacist in Charge (PIC). If one tablet goes missing, there is no need to fill out this form.

-DEA Form 222: This form is used to purchase and return outdated Schedule II (C-II) drugs only. This form comes available in three colors:

- Blue Copy- The purchaser (Pharmacy) keeps this copy on file for at least two years. The pharmacy is the purchaser until they are returning outdated C-II drugs. When returning C-II drugs, the pharmacy becomes the seller.

- Green Copy- The seller (wholesaler, most times) sends this copy to the local DEA.

- Brown Copy- The seller (wholesaler, most times) keeps this copy on file.

-DEA Form 224: This form is used for a pharmacy to dispense controlled substances and obtain a DEA number.

-DEA Form 225: This form is needed to manufacture and dispense controlled substances. A DEA number is obtained for this purpose.

-DEA Form 363: This form is needed to operate as a controlled substance abuse treatment program or to compound controlled substance medications.

<u>Medication Recalls</u>

When a medication recall occurs, the pharmacy is notified and asked to check for specific lot numbers and expiration dates that have been identified as affected medications.

- **Class I Recall:** Attempts to notify patients that a drug could cause serious harm or death.

- **Class II Recall:** Pharmacy is notified that a drug has consistency issues with potency. The patient does not need to be notified. The probability of serious harm is not likely and the effects with the drug may be temporary or reversible.

- **Class III Recall:** Manufacture and Pharmacy level only. The public or patient does not need to be notified. Not likely to cause any serious effects or harm.

Controlled Substances Schedules

When the Drug Enforcement Administration (DEA) was formed, it was determined that controlled substances or medications with a high potential of abuse needed to be placed in categories or "schedules." This enacted the Comprehensive Drug Abuse Prevention and Control Act of 1970 (CSA of 1970). Scheduled medication have a federal warning against sharing these types of medications with a non-prescribed patient. Failure to abide by this law may result in fines and/ or criminal charges. The schedules are categorized from highest abuse potential to lowest abuse potential, use the letter "C" and roman numerals of I, II, III, IV, and V.

Controlled Substances Schedules

Below, each schedule is listed with its potential of abuse/medical use level, prescription expiration date, refill possibilities, and medication examples from each schedule

Schedules	Medical Use	Prescription Expiration Date	Refills	Medication Examples
Schedule One (C-I)	None	Illegal	Illegal	Herion, LSD, Marijuana, and Mescaline (etc.)
Schedule Two (C-II) *Must use DEA Form 222 for ordering and returning*	Limited, may lead to high abuse (server dependance)	30 days	None	Amphetamine, Cocaine, Codeine, Fentanyl, Hydromorphone, Methadone, Morphine, Methylphenidate, Lortab, Norco, Opium, and Oxycodone (etc.)
Schedule Three (C-III) *Order using a purchasing invoice*	Allowed (abuse potential is less than C-I and C-II)	6 months	Max: 5 refills	Anabolic Steroids, Cough Syrups containing Hydrocodone, Suboxone, and Tylenol #3, (etc.)
Schedule Four (C-IV) *Order using a purchasing invoice*	Allowed (abuse potential is less than, C-I, C-II, and C-III)	6 months	Max: 5 refills	Alprazolam, Diazepam, Lorazepam, Phentermine, and Phenobarbital (etc.)
Schedule Five (C-V) *Order using a purchasing invoice*	Allowed (abuse potential is less than, C-I, C-II, C-III, and C-IV)	6 months	Max: 5 refills	Robatussin AC, Promethazine VC w/ Codeine, and Lyrica (etc.)

Pharmacy Resources

- **Orange Book: Approved Drugs Products with Therapeutic Equivalence Evaluations**- The Orange Book compares whether a certain medication can be substituted in place of another medication using an "A or B" rating system. Medications rated A can be substituted because they are bioequivalent. Medications rated B can **NOT** be substituted because they are **NOT** bioequivalent. This book is also called "FDA's Approved Drug Product Publication" and it is published yearly.

- **Red Book: Drug Topics Red Book**- This book provides a listing of medications by manufacturers, brand, generic, strength, size, and price.

- **Purple Book: Physician's Desk Reference (PDR)**- This book contains package insert information for medications and is widely used by physicians. This book is published yearly and has colorful pictures of medications along with the manufacturers address and phone number.

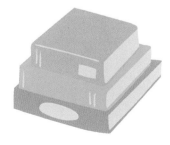

Practice Exam

1. When ordering C-III through C-V medications you need the following form?
A. DEA Form 222
B. DEA Form 106
C. DEA Form 203
D. Purchasing Invoice

2. The red copy of the DEA Form 222 needs to be sent to this office?
A. Local DEA office
B. Federal DEA office
C. There is no red copy. Only blue, green, and brown
D. Local police station in case of theft

3. Federal, how many grams of pseudoephedrine is a patient able to purchase on a Monday?
A. 12 grams
B. 3.6 grams
C. 9 grams
D. 7.5 grams

4. The Physician Desk Reference is also known as this book?
A. Purple Book
B. Approved Pricing Book
C. Package Insert Book
D. American Index Book

5. When following pharmacy law between federal and state, this is the law you should reference?
A. HIPAA
B. State Law
C. Federal Law
D. The law that is the strictest

6. Schedule Two (C-II) has ____ refills, and expires in _____?
A. Zero, 6 months
B. Zero, 30 days
C. Five, 1 calendar year
D. Eleven, 30 days

7. Mescaline is an example of a Schedule_____?
A. 5
B. 4
C. 3
D. 1

8. When ordering or returning a Schedule Two (C-II), you should use this form?
A. DEA Form 106
B. DEA Form 222
C. DEA Form 363
D. DEA Form 41

9. Schedule Four (C-IV) has ___ abuse potential than C-I, C-II, and C-III.
A. More
B. Less
C. Equally
D. Allowed

10. Which statement is true about NDC numbers?
A. The last segment (3rd segment) represents the manufacturer
B. The NDC number is printed on the inside of the medication bottle
C. The middle segment (2nd segment) is the medication product information
D. All of these are true

11. This type of recall the Pharmacist must reach out to the patient, but the patient will not have any serious adverse reactions?
A. Class 5
B. Class 2
C. Class 1
D. Schedule 4

12. A list of medication package inserts could be in which of these books?
A. Drug Topics
B. Physician Desk Reference
C. American Index
D. Facts and Comparison

13. Nurses are allowed to order all types of medications except for this one?
A. Vicodin
B. Cocaine
C. LSD
D. Phentermine

14. You and your Pharmacist report to work and discover that all the Schedule Two (C-II) and Schedule Fours (C-IV) are missing. What form will you fill out to report this?

A. DEA Form 106
B. DEA Form Blue
C. DEA Form 222
D. DEA Form 41

15. Your pharmacy sells 100 Adderall tablets per month. During the inventory counts, you discover that 3 tablets are missing. What should you do?

A. Fill out a DEA Form 106
B. Notify the local police and local DEA
C. Both A and B
D. Nothing, because 5% of the yearly total is not missing.

16. Promethazine is an example of which schedule?
A. C-IV
B. C-V
C. C-I
D. Promethazine is not a schedule

17. If someone wants to start a treatment center for controlled substance abuse, which DEA Form should they fill out?
A. DEA Form 225
B. DEA Form 363
C. DEA Form 41
D. DEA Form 222

18. What is the max number of refills allowed on C-III through C-V in 6 months?

A. 10 refills
B. 6 refills,
C. No refills
D. 5 refills

19. Who can order C-I controlled substances?
A. No one
B. Physician
C. Physician Assistant
D. Registered Nurse

20. Which of the following medications must be dispensed with a package insert?
A. Premarin
B. Esomeprazole
C. Accutane
D. Metoprolol

21. The segments of a NDC number represent the following:
A. Manufacture, drug information, drug strength
B. Drug information, package size, expiration date
C. Manufacture, drug information, package size
D. Package size, dosage form, expiration date

22. This type of medication recall must go to the patient level?
A. Class 1
B. Class 2
C. Class 3
D. Class 4

23. What is the total number of tablets, if a patient is dispensed 90 tablets with 3 refills?
A. 90 tablets
B. 180 tablets
C. 270 tablets
D. 360 tablets

24. A prescription for Methylphenidate comes into the pharmacy. The signa code says: Take one table by mouth b.i.d, one before school and one before homework. The dispense was 90 tablets, 2 refills. What is wrong with this prescription?

A. Nothing, the prescription is ready to be filled
B. The quantity is too high
C. There should not be any refills
D. Both C and B

25. A prescription for Oxycodone comes into the pharmacy. The signa code says: Take one table by mouth daily. The dispense was 10 tablets, 2 refills. What is wrong with this prescription?

A. The quantity is too low
B. There should not be any refills
C. Both A and B
D. Nothing, the prescription is ready to be filled

26. Accutane and Intrauterine contraceptives should be dispensed with:
A. Warning labels
B. Package inserts
C. Copays
D. On separate occasions

27. Which drug does not require child proof packaging?
A. Acetaminophen
B. Nitrospan
C. Norepinephrine
D. Oral Contraceptive

28. This act established the difference between behind the counter and over the counter medications?
A. Food, Drug, and Cosmetic Act of 1938
B. CSA of 1970
C. Durham Humphrey Amendment of 1951
D. Kefauver- Harris Amendment of 1962

29. This act allows low-cost transmission of insurance claims and protects patient privacy health information?
A. HIPPA
B. HIPAA
C. HMO
D. HOA

30. What year did the FDA regulate the unadulterated and mislabeling of cosmetics?
A. 2006
B. 1996
C. 1906
D. 1938

31. This act is also known as the Pure Food and Drug Act?
A. Kefauver-Harris Amendment of 1962
B. FDA of 1906
C. FDCA of 1938
D. Obamacare 2010

32. This act limited the transportation and purchase of Opium in the United States?
A. Durham Humphrey Amendment of 1951
B. Kefauver-Harris Amendment of 1962
C. Comprehensive Drug Abuse Prevention of 1970
D. Harris Narcotic Act of 1914

33. The Comprehensive Drug Abuse Prevention created what new process?
A. Fair pricing of brand and generic drugs
B. Placed controlled substances into schedules
C. Child Proof packaging
D. Orphan drugs

34. What act helped create the career field for Pharmacy Technicians?
A. OBRA 90
B. HIPAA 1996
C. Dietary Supplements of 1994
D. Food and Drug Administration Act of 1988

35. Dietary supplements that are not under the supervision of physician must have the following on its label?
A. No false claims
B. Active Ingredients
C. Inactive Ingredients
D. All the above

36. What does the FDA consider a false claim to be?
A. Medications claiming to treat an illness, but does not
B. Adverse Reactions
C. Drug to Drug interactions not discovered during drug trials
D. Testing on animals, but claim to work on humans

37. This law was created to offer incentive to manufacturers that created generic drugs and extended patents of existing medications?
A. Harrison Narcotic Amendment
B. Durham Humphrey Amendment
C. OBRA 90
D. Hatch-Waxman Amendment

38. What law requires an attempt to offer counseling to Medicaid patients or patients with a new prescription?
A. FDA 1906
B. Orphan Drugs Act 1983
C. HIPAA 1996
D. OBRA 90

39. Orphan drugs are for the following;
A. Children without parents
B. Small group of the population with rare diseases
C. Research only
D. Medicaid patients

40. What year was the FDA agency "established" as a part of the Department of Health and Human Services?
A. 2010
B. 1988
C. 1938
D. 1906

41. If a patient comes in and purchases 9 grams of pseudoephedrine on September 3rd, 2022, when will the patient be able to purchase the next 3.6 grams?
A. The next day
B. The following week
C. 30 days
D. Never

42. CMEA stands for:
A. Contained Morphine Enhance Act
B. Controlled Methamphetamine Epidemic Act
C. Controlled Methamphetamine Evolution Act
D. Controlled Metformin Established Act

43. This act allowed medications to seek approval faster and required all manufacturers bottles to place an "Rx only" symbol on their bottles?
A. Food and Drug Modernization Act of 1997
B. Omnibus Budget Reconciliation Act of 1990
C. Hatch-Waxman Amendment of 1984
D. Food, Drug, and Cosmetic Act of 1938

44. A prescription pads is required to have tamper proof paper and/or symbols because of this law?
A. Medicaid 2010
B. Medicaid Tamper 2008
C. Obamacare 2010
D. Pure Food Act 1906

45. This act allowed every American to receive affordable health insurance regardless of any pre-existing medical conditions?
A. Hatch-Waxman Amendment of 1984
B. Obamacare 2010
C. Affordable Insurance Act
D. Durham Humphrey Amendment

46. Hatch- Waxman Amendment of 1984 is also known as:
A. Marijuana Law
B. Birth Control Law
C. Schedule One Restoration Act
D. Drug Price Competition Act

47. An older patient with heart problems has made a request that their Nitroglycerin be placed in child proof packaging because they babysit their four-year-old granddaughter often. Is this allowed?

A. Yes, the patient is concerned about the child's safety
B. No, the child is not five years old
C. No, Nitroglycerin is federally not allowed to be placed in childproof packaging
D. Yes, the patient can get what they want

48. When a drug is recalled, the Pharmacy Technician must remove the medication from inventory by looking for this?
A. Drug Name and Strength
B. Lot Number and Expiration Date
C. Batch Number and NDC number
D. The Green DEA Form 222

49. A patient that wants to purchase pseudoephedrine must present this for the purchase?
A. Passport
B. Social Security Number
C. Medicaid Part D card
D. Driver's License or State Identification Card

50. The Sherley Amendment of 1912 was the first law in place to prohibit false therapeutic claims?
A. True
B. False

51. This amendment was enacted due to birth defect in Europe because patients were on this medication while pregnant?
A. Hydrochlorothiazide
B. Thalidomide
C. Cyclophosphamide
D. Benazepril

52. Manufactures are required to register annually, report adverse reactions, be inspected every two years, and must prove their medications are safe and effective because of this amendment?
A. Hatch-Waxman
B. Durham Humphrey
C. Kefauver-Harris
D. Sherley Amendment

53. This act defined mislabeling and required manufacturers to alert that the medication "may be habit forming"
A. Food, Drug, and Cosmetic Act of 1938
B. Food and Drug Act of 1906
C. Food and Drug Administration Act of 1988
D. FDA Modernization Act of 1997

54. The Food and Drug Administration Act banned this?
A. Sample drugs being sold or trade
B. Deep discounts for hospitals
C. Both A and B
D. Answer not available

55. Drug Utilization Reviews are a major part of this law?
A. HIPPA 1996
B. HIPAA 1995
C. OBRA 90
D. FDA 1988

56. Patient specific medication labels must have all the following, except:
A. Pharmacy Address
B. Physician DEA number
C. Patient name
D. Expiration date

57. Patient medication labels are a part of this law that was enacted?
A. Food and Drug Act of 1906
B. Kefauver-Harris Amendment of 1962
C. Food, Drug, and Cosmetic Act of 1938
D. Dietary Supplement Health and Education Act of 1994

58. Clinical Pharmacology, Adverse Reaction, and Overdose information are examples of information that can be found on the patients _____?
A. Package Insert
B. Leaflet
C. Computer Profile
D. Medication label

59. It is federal law that manufacturers must have one of these on all manufacturers behind the counter medication bottles?
A. May be habit forming
B. Please consult your Physician or Pharmacist
C. NDC number
D. Rx only

60. The FDA took control of monitoring these types of labels in 1994?
A. Dietary Supplements
B. Over the counter medications
C. Behind the counter medications
D. Both A and C

Answer Key

1.	D	16.	D
2.	C	17.	B
3.	B	18.	D
4.	A	19.	A
5.	D	20.	C
6.	B	21.	C
7.	D	22.	A
8.	B	23.	D
9.	B	24.	D
10.	C	25.	B
11.	B	26.	B
12.	B	27.	B
13.	C	28.	C
14.	A	29.	B
15.	D	30.	D

Answer Key

31.	B	46.	D
32.	D	47.	C
33.	B	48.	B
34.	A	49.	D
35.	D	50.	A
36.	A	51.	B
37.	D	52.	C
38.	D	53	A
39.	B	54.	C
40.	B	55.	C
41.	C	56.	B
42.	B	57.	C
43	A	58.	A
44.	B	59.	D
45.	B	60.	A

Final Thoughts

The time between this book and my first book, "The Pharmacy Technician Exam Review" was 2 days. If I do say myself, that was quite quick. But that shows my love for Pharmacy and being a Certified Pharmacy Technician. I am a woman from Detroit, living in New Orleans, dodging hurricanes, raising two sons (Mikal, 14; and Israel, 2), and wishing for every future Pharmacy Technician to become successfully in all areas of pharmacy. That is all, folks!!! That is who Sharon Denise Garrett is. My mother asked me how I felt when I wrote my first book and I informed her I did not feel any type of way. But the positive responses from my students, colleagues, and other healthcare workers has finally hit me. I have wanted to become a writer since I was in the 6th grade. My cousin, *Ashley D. Brown* of Detroit, Michigan; reminded me of this yesterday on Facebook. And now, here I am. I hope that this book is helpful to you and your success. If you have any questions or just want to say hello, I can be emailed at: ***gpsrxla@gmail.com***. Happy reading and good luck with your exam!!! - Sharon D. Garrett, CPhT

<u>About the author:</u>

Sharon D. Garrett is a Pharmacy Technician Program Director in New Orleans, Louisiana. She has been a Certified Pharmacy Technician for the past 14 years, starting in 2008 in Detroit, Michigan. She has two sons Mikal and Israel. Sharon is a member of multiple national Pharmacy organizations and advisory boards. In January 2022, her simulated labs were featured on the PTCB.org website. Her main goal is to help those that want to become Pharmacy Technicians. This is her second book, her first book being: "*<u>The Pharmacy Technicians Exam Review</u>*".

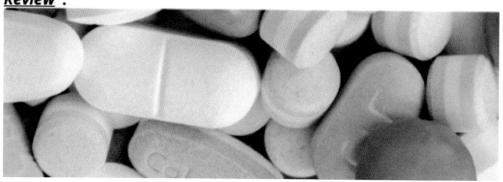

Made in the USA
Monee, IL
08 October 2022